ABOUT THE PHOTOGRAPHER & CREATOR

HI, MY NAME IS AMANDA AND I CREATED THIS COLORING BOOK FROM EDITED AND STYLIZED PHOTOS FROM MY PORTFOLIO.

IN ADDITION TO TAKING PHOTOS, I ALSO ENJOY WRITING, HIKING, EXPLORING NEW PLACES, AND LEARNING NEW THINGS.

I TAKE PHOTOS OF EVERYTHING, BUT LANDSCAPES AND BEAUTIFUL SPACES ARE MY FAVORITE.

THANK YOU FOR SUPPORTING MY PASSION FOR ART!

Amanda

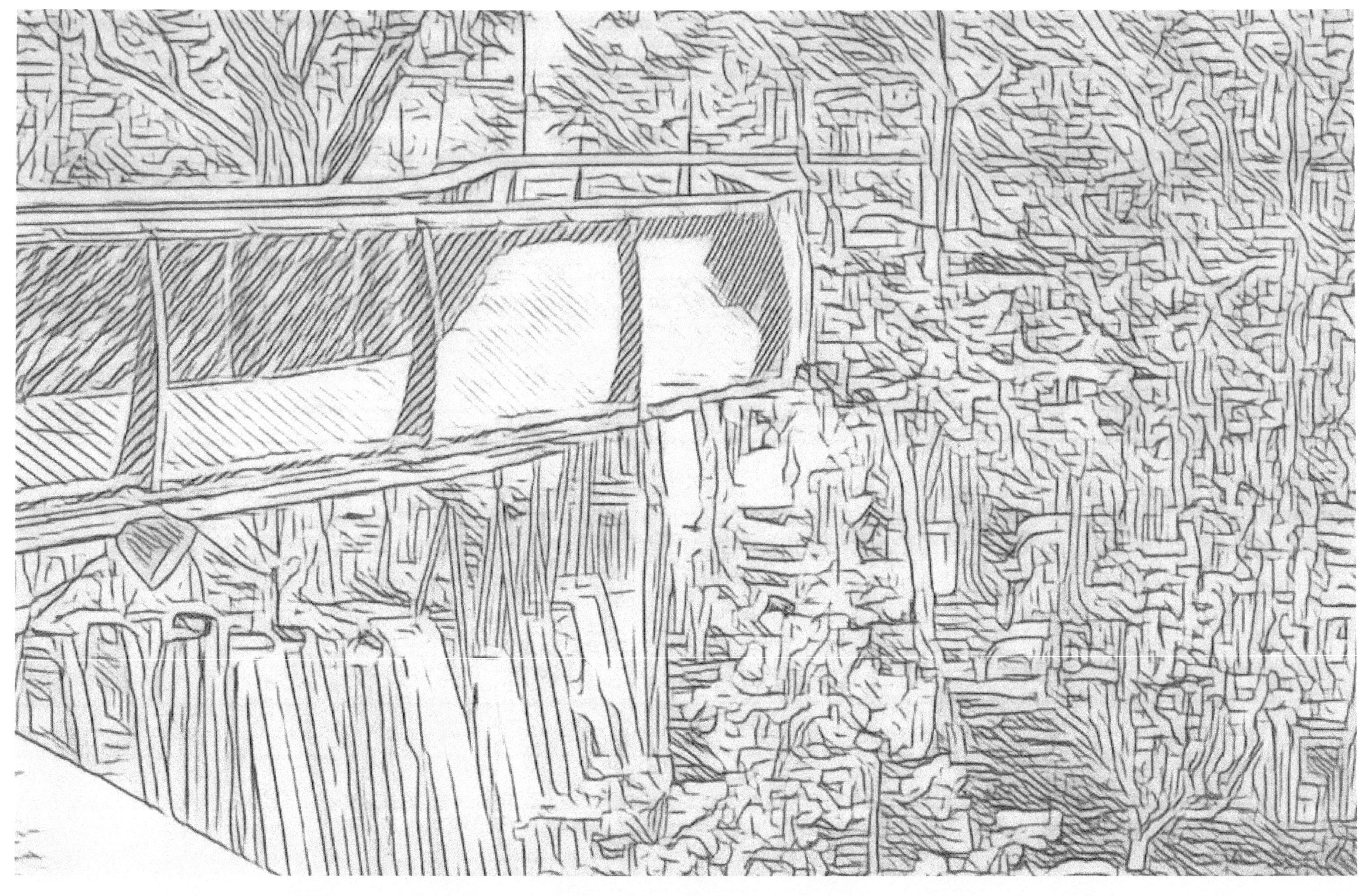

WALKING BRIDGE AT PROMENADE PARK

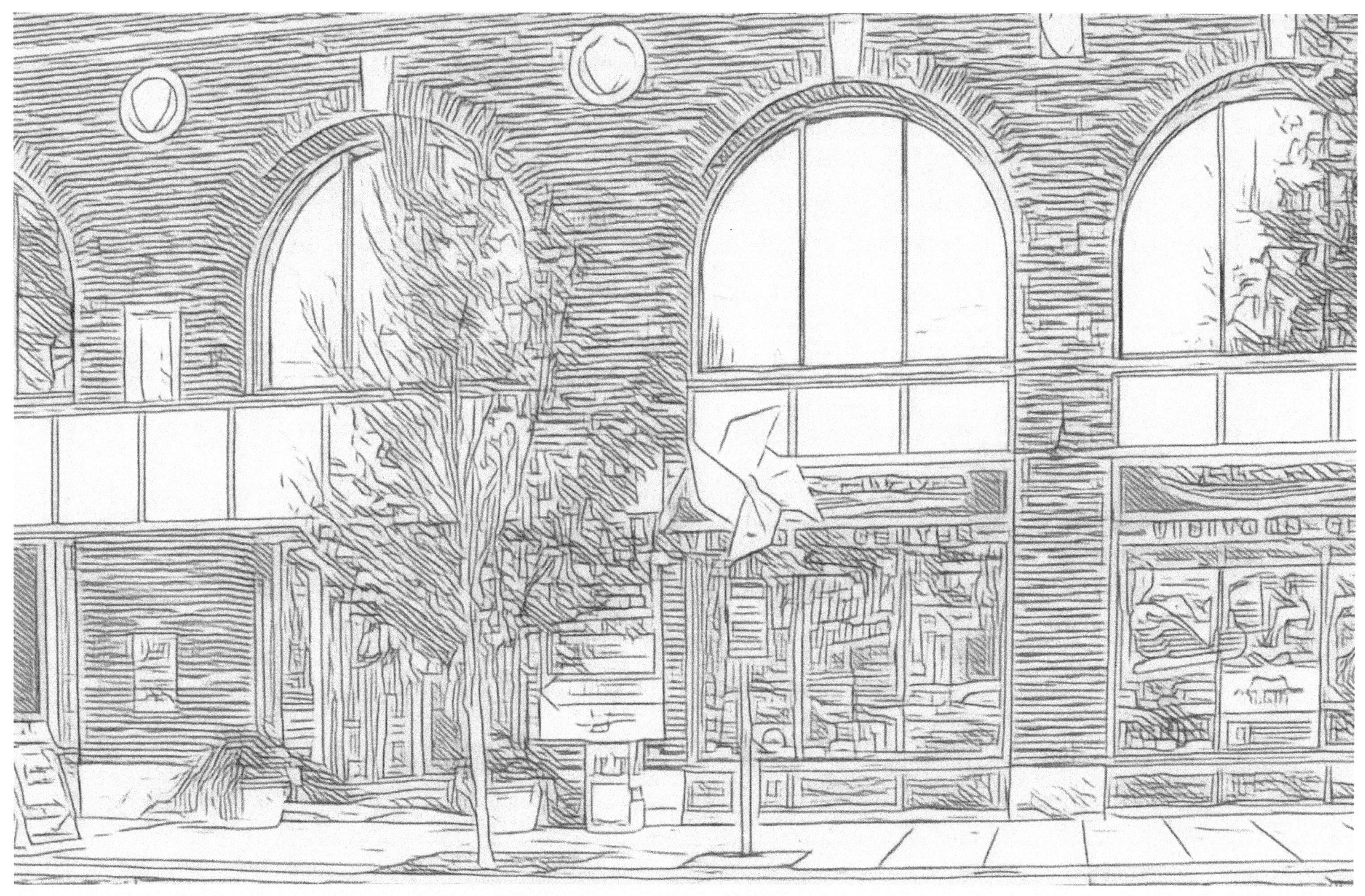

VISIT FORT WAYNE
927 S HARRISON ST, FORT WAYNE, IN 46802

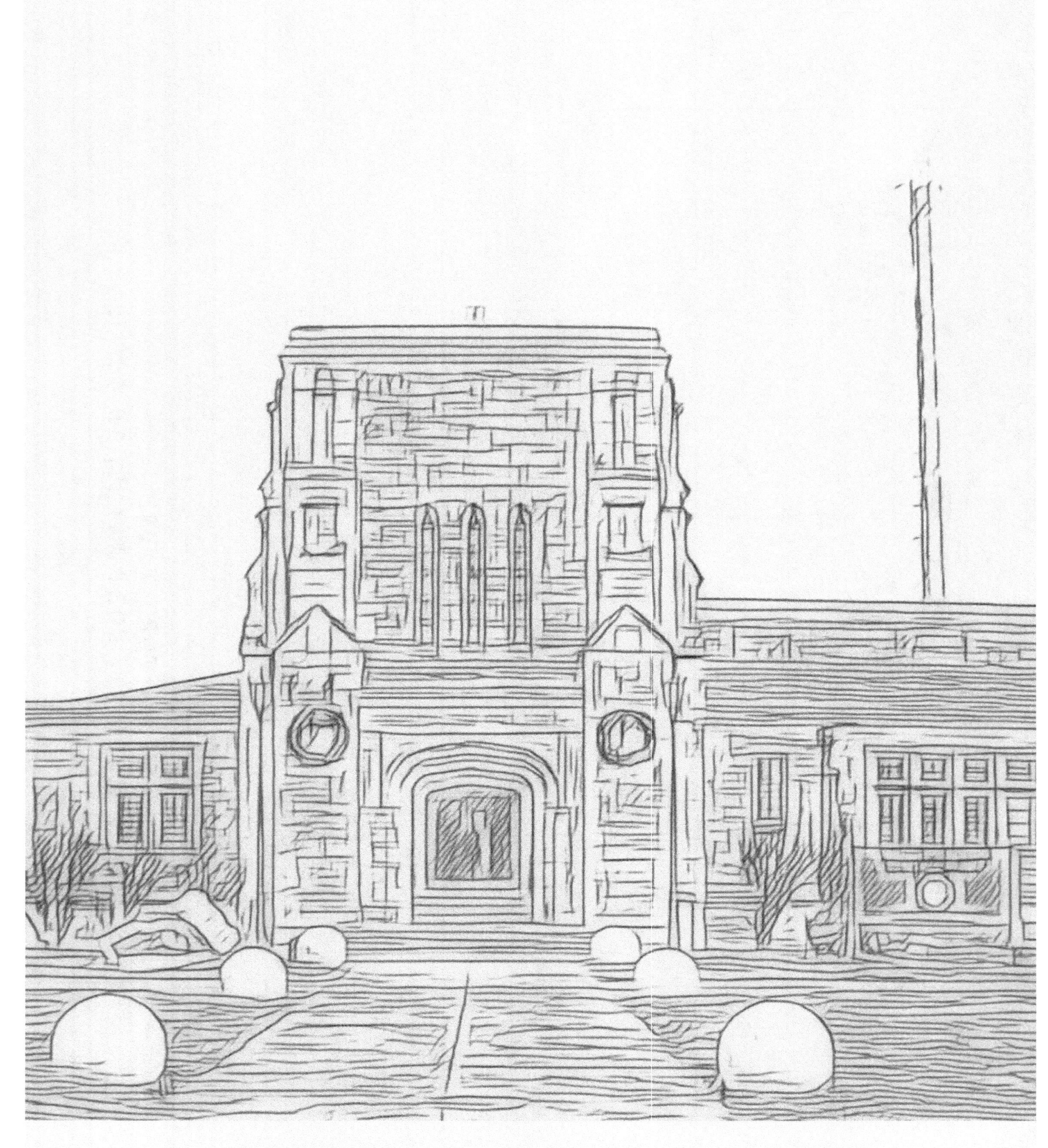

FORT WAYNE WATER FILTRATION
1100 GRISWOLD DR, FORT WAYNE 46805

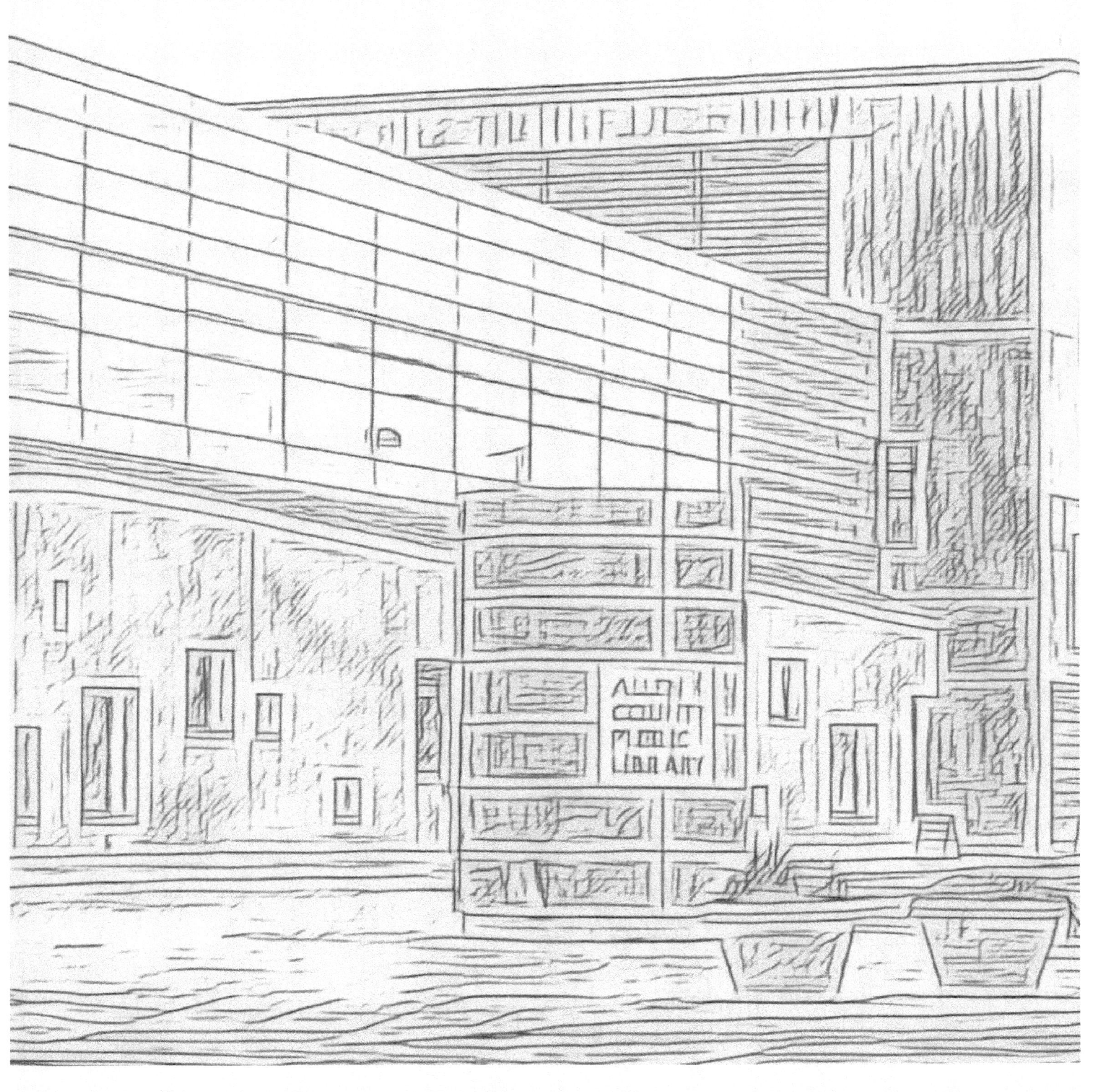

ALLEN COUNTY PUBLIC LIBRARY
900 LIBRARY PLAZA, FORT WAYNE, IN 46802

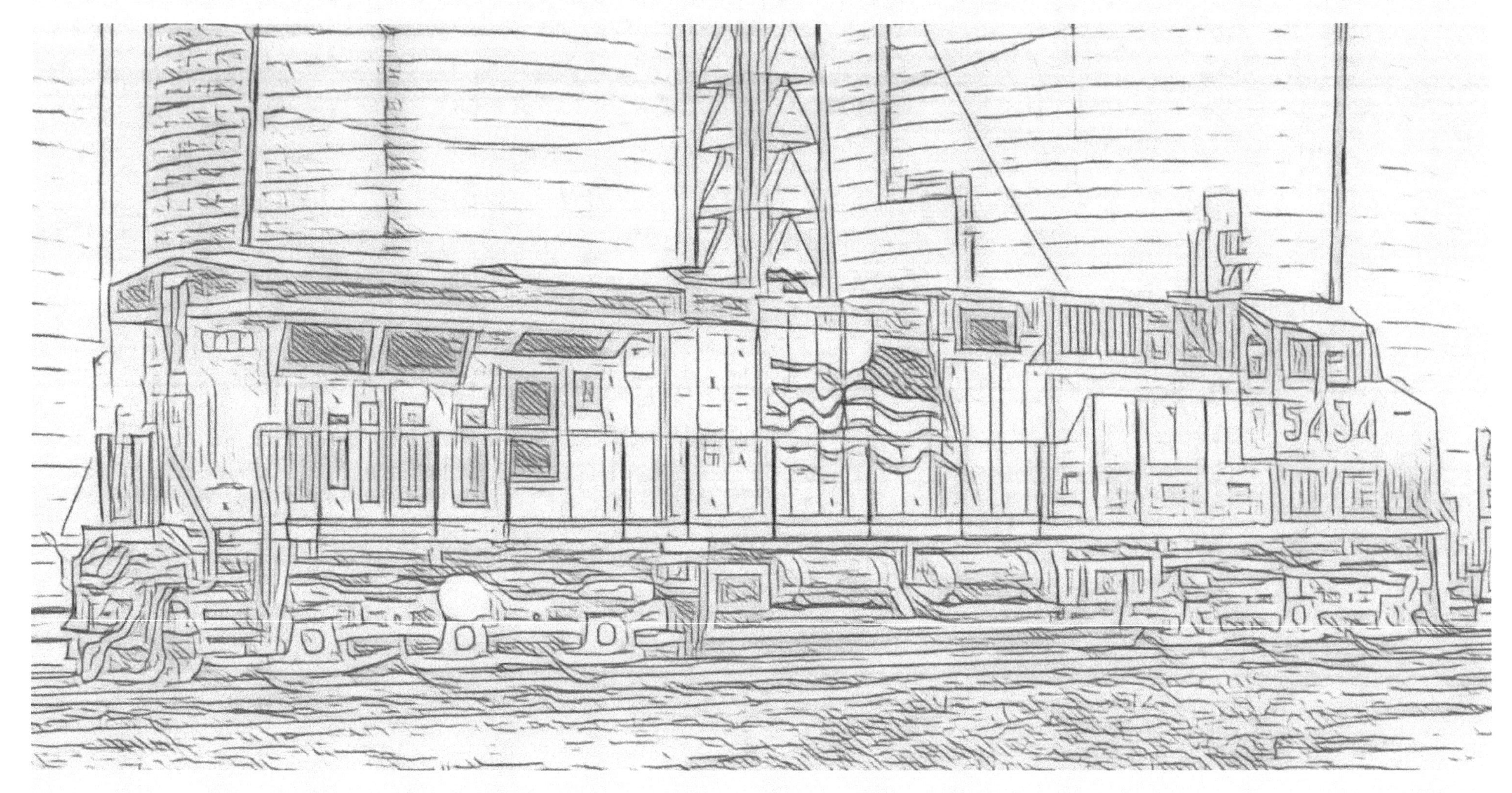

NORFOLK SOUTHERN RAILWAY WAST WAYNE YARD
8111 NELSON RD, FORT WAYNE, IN 46803

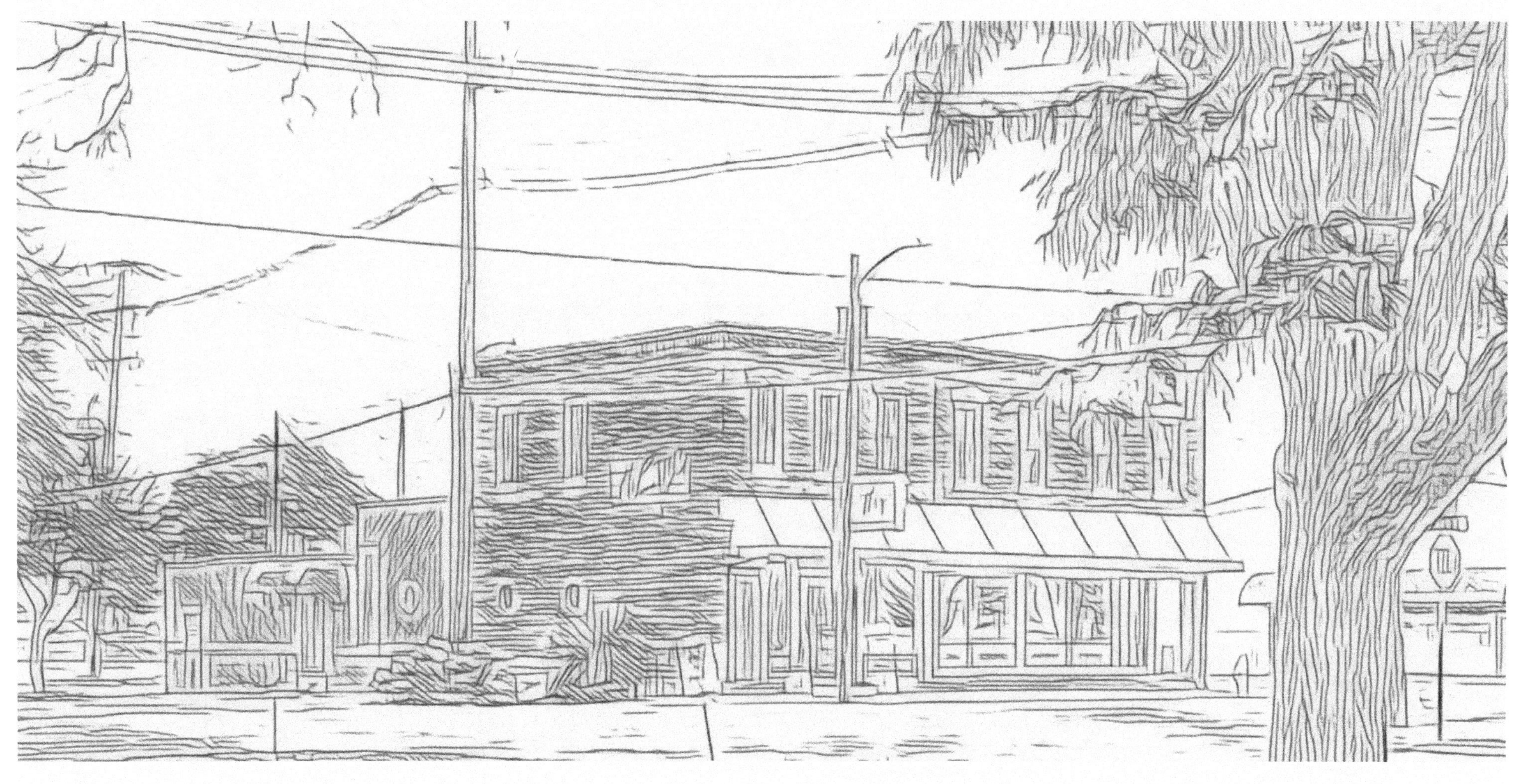

HENRY'S, 536 W MAIN ST, FORT WAYNE, IN 46802

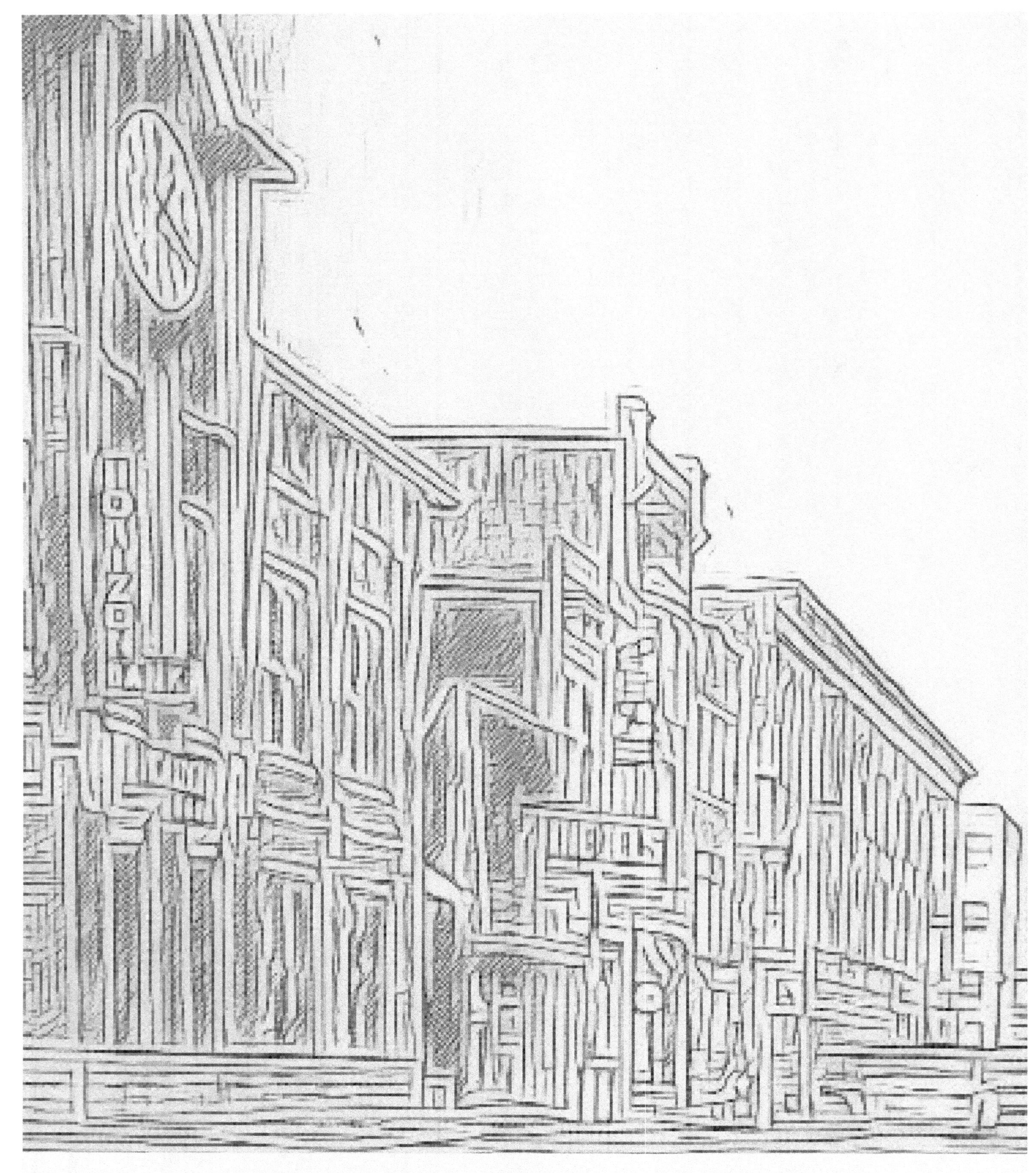

RIEGEL'S PIPE AND TOBACCO SHOP
624 CALHOUN ST, FORT WAYNE, IN 46802

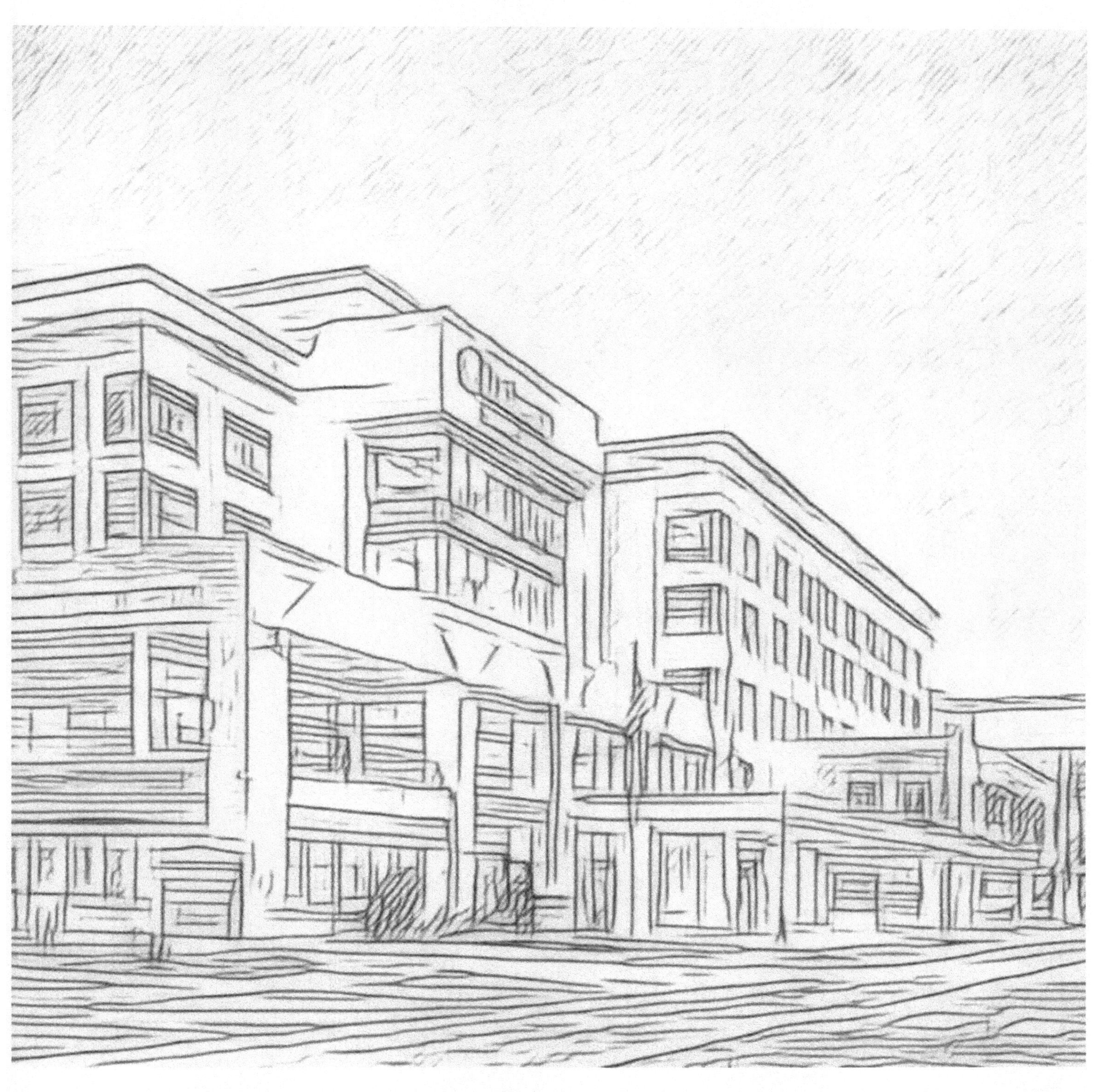

LUTHERAN DOWNTOWN HOSPITAL
702 VAN BUREN ST, FORT WAYNE, IN 46802

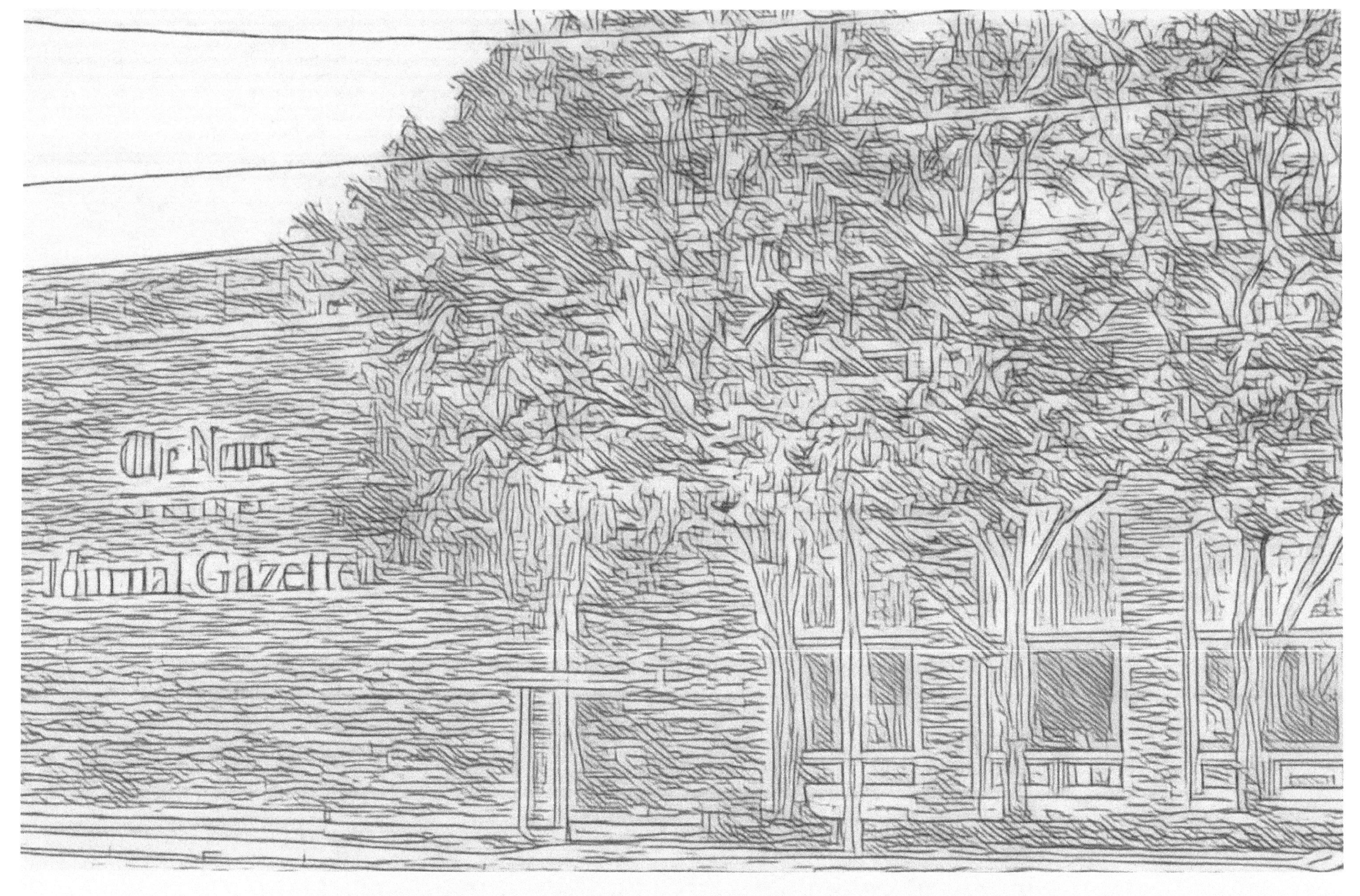

THE NEWS SENTINEL & THE JOURNAL GAZETTE
600 W. MAIN ST., FORT WAYNE, IN 46802

THE HISTORIC SWINNEY HOMESTEAD
1424 W. JEFFERSON BLVD. FORT WAYNE, INDIANA 46802

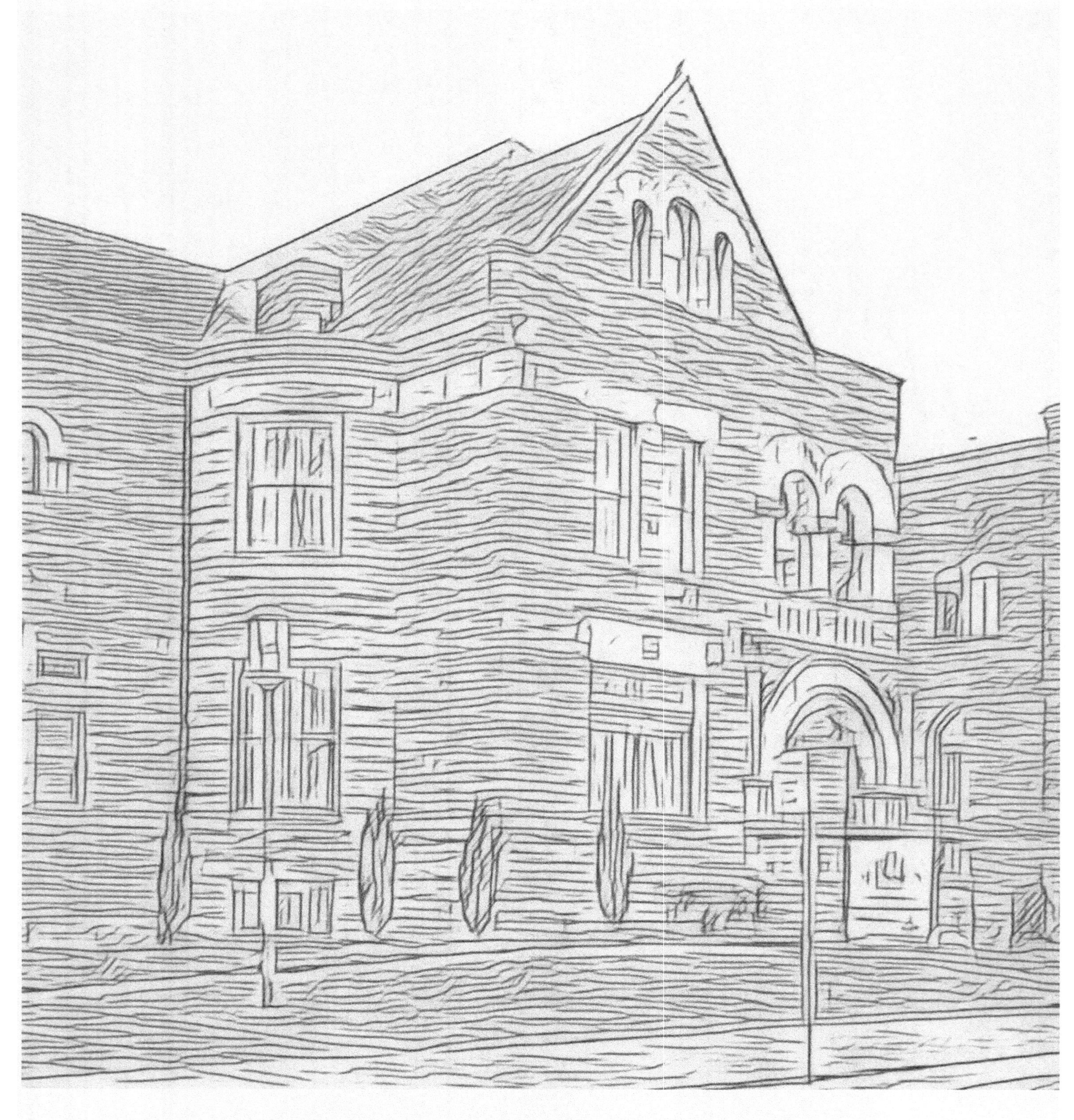

THE BELL MANSION
420 W WAYNE ST, FORT WAYNE, IN 46802

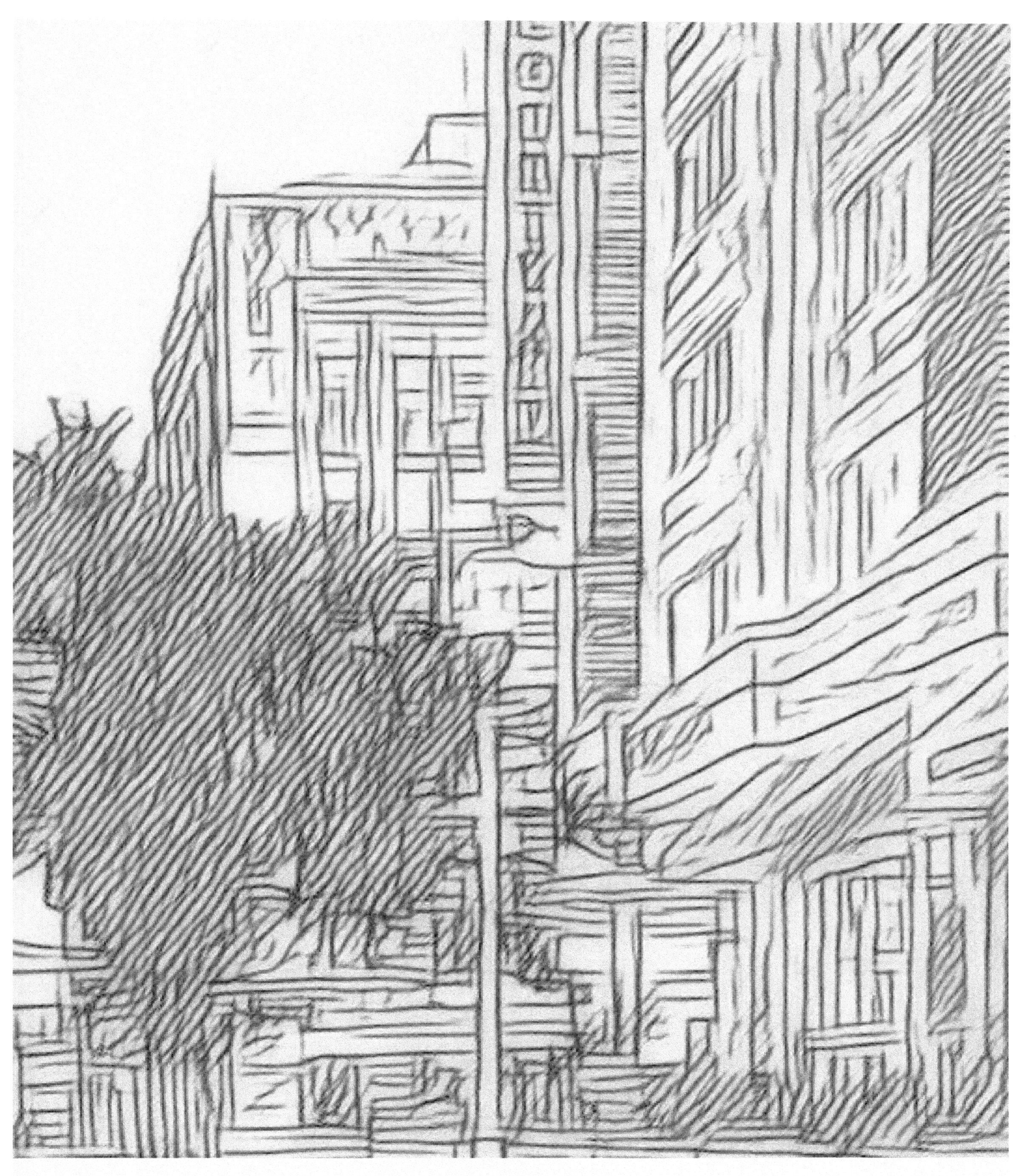

COURTYARD BY MARRIOTT
1150 S HARRISON ST, FORT WAYNE, IN 46802

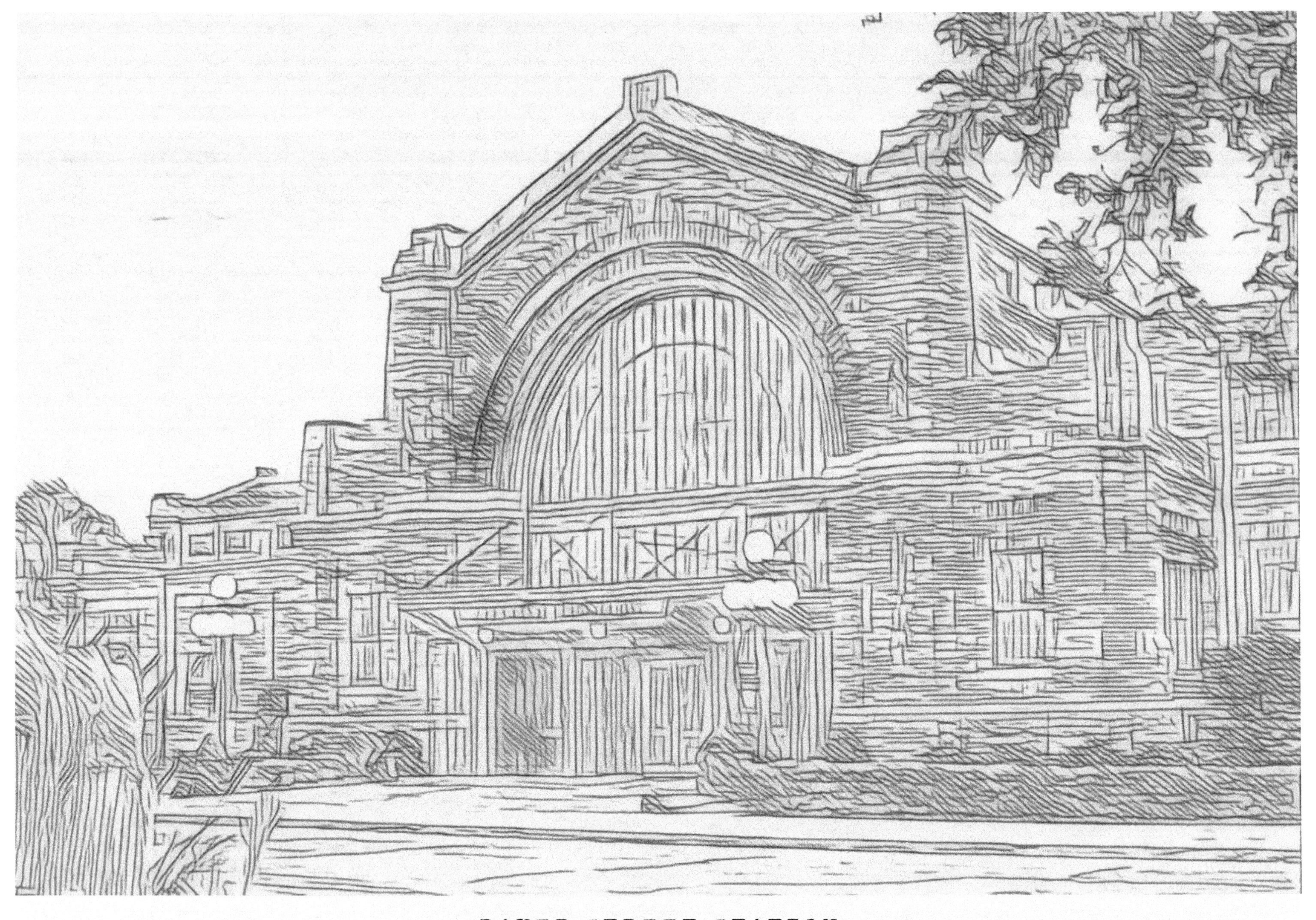

BAKER STREET STATION
221 W BAKER ST, FORT WAYNE, IN 46802

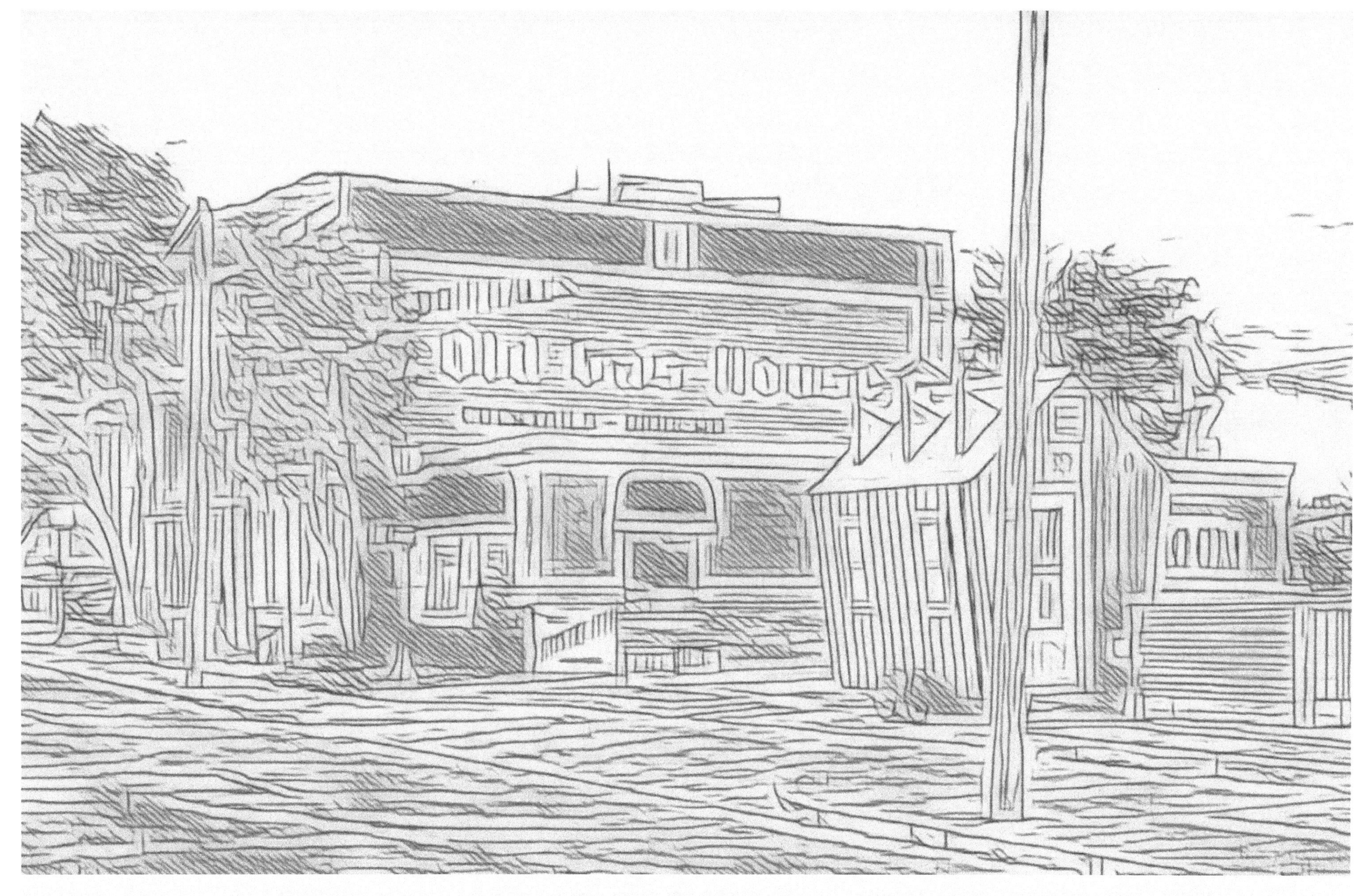

DON HALL'S OLD GAS HOUSE & TAKAOKA OF JAPAN
305 E SUPERIOR ST, FORT WAYNE, IN 46802

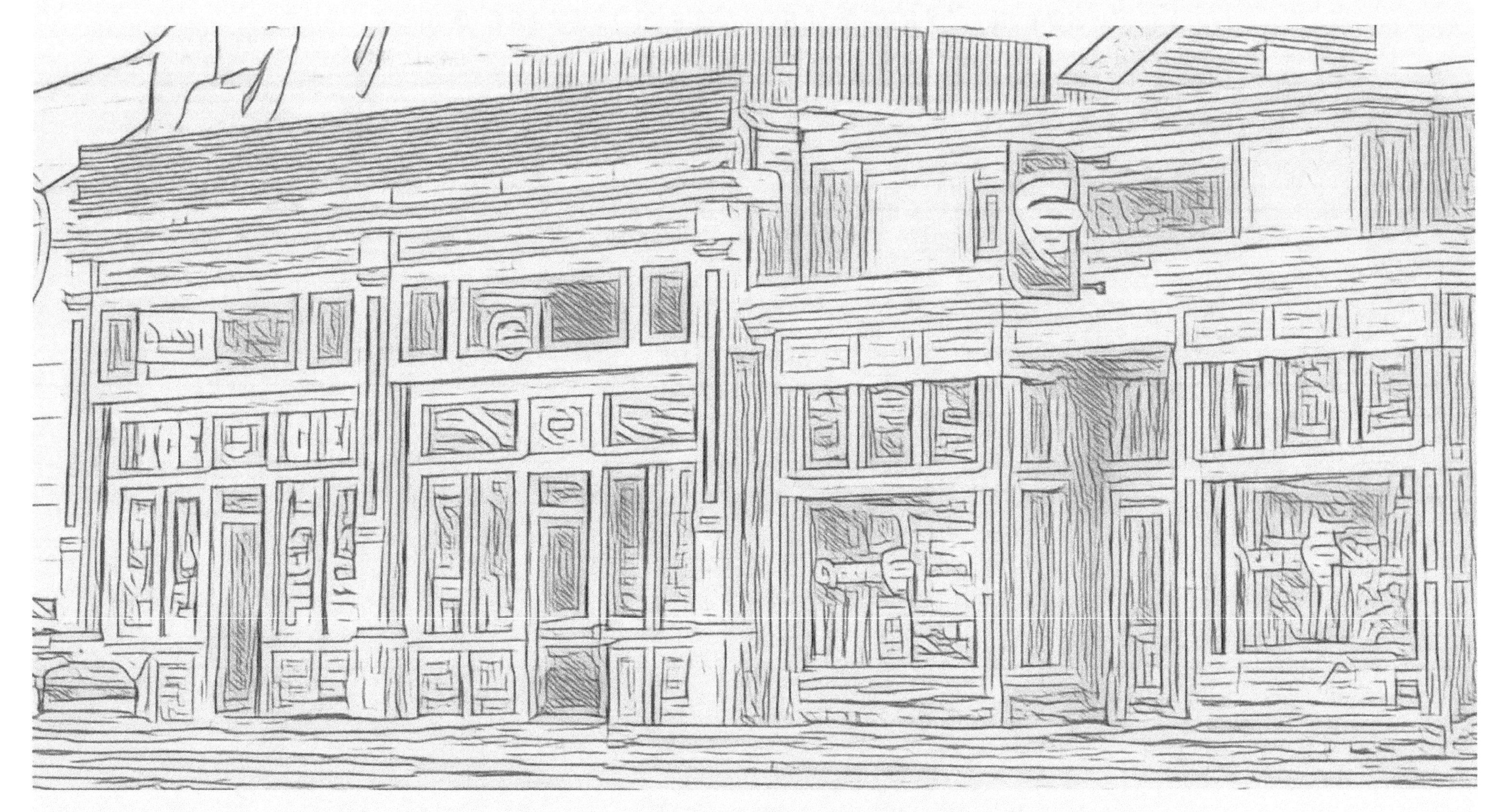

SWEETS ON MAIN & CYCLONE SOCIAL
W MAIN ST, FORT WAYNE, IN 46802

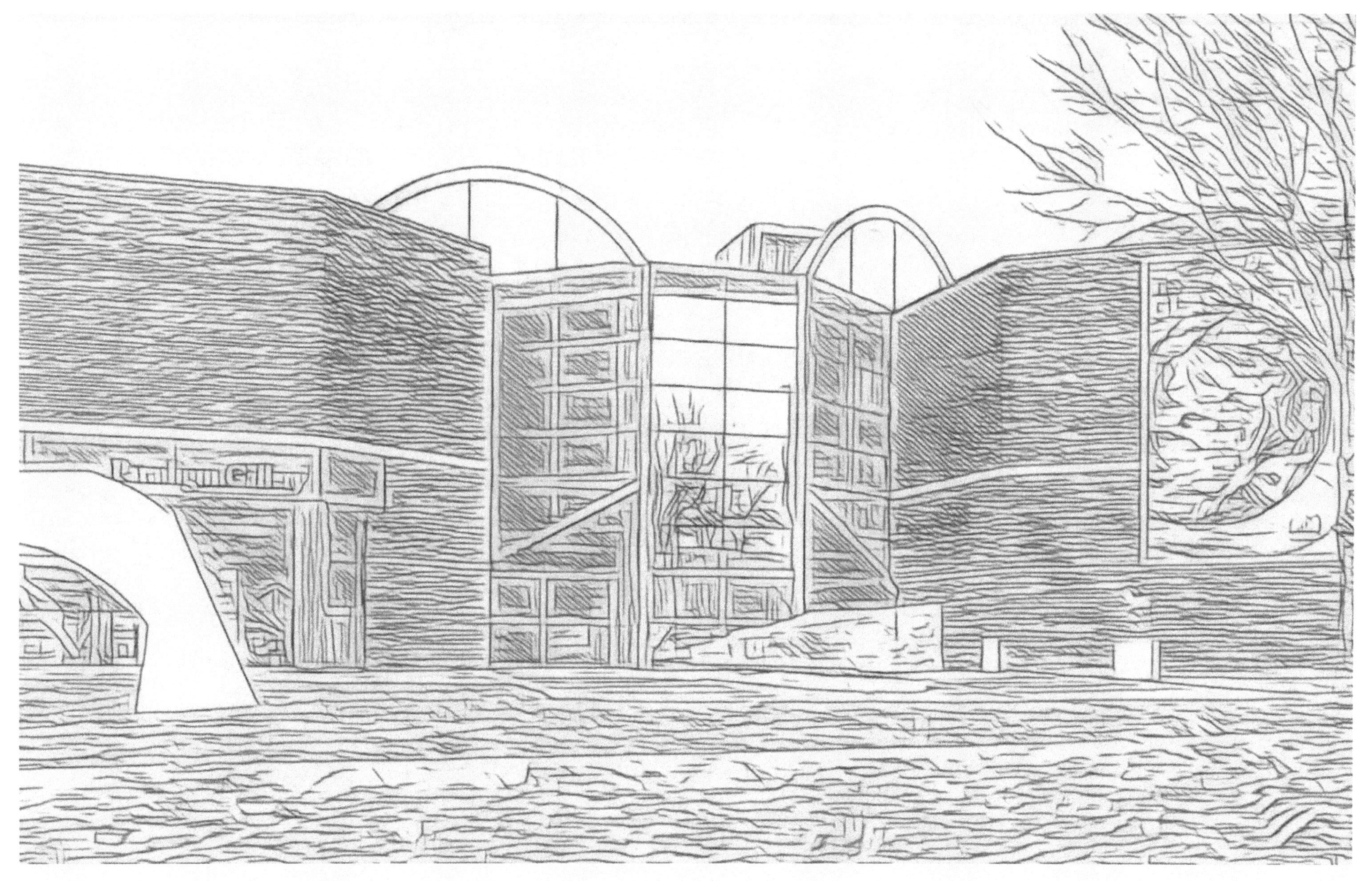

FORT WAYNE MUSEUM OF ART
311 E MAIN ST, FORT WAYNE, IN 46802

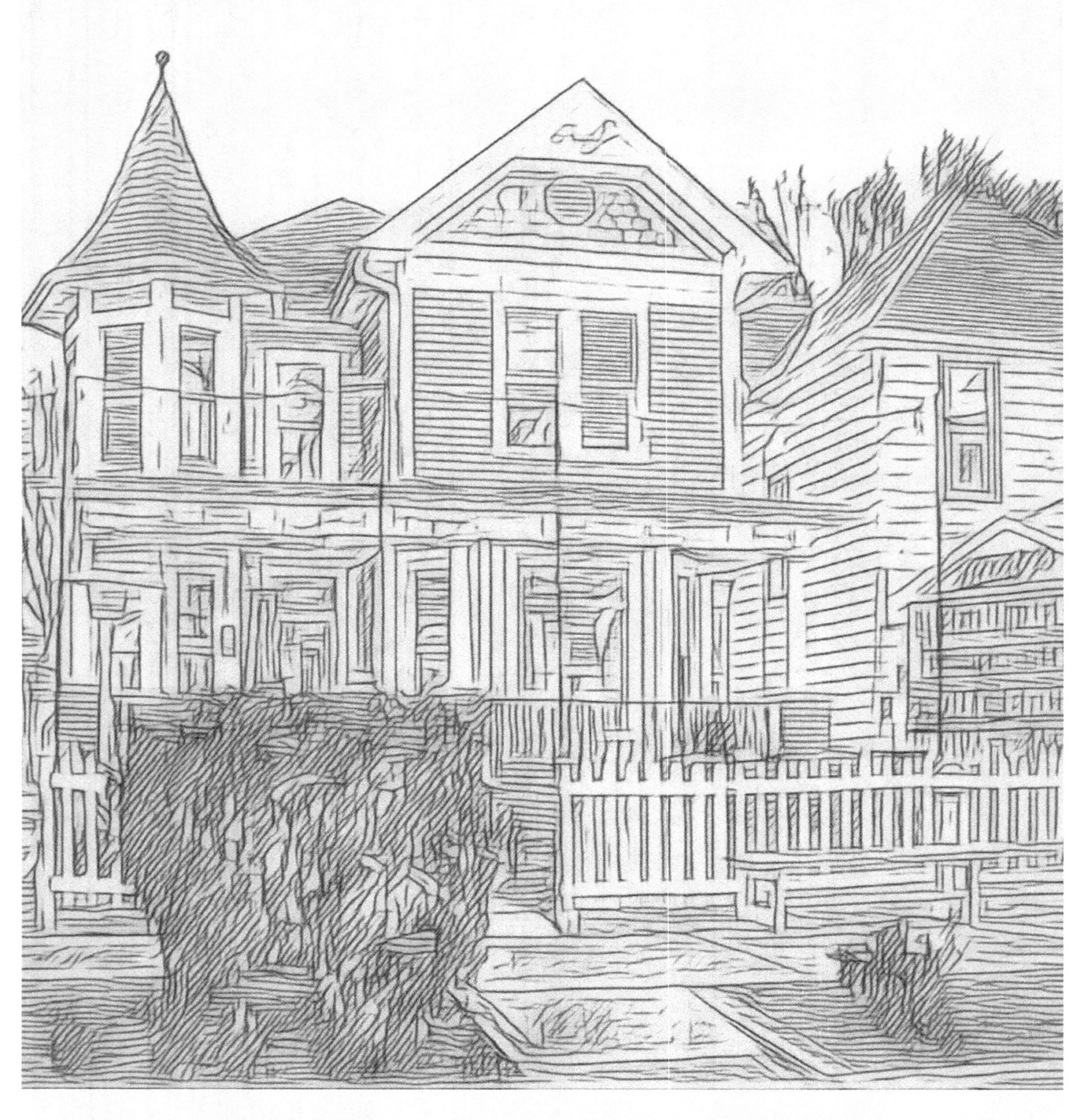

RUDY'S
3313 409 BRACKENRIDGE ST, FORT WAYNE, IN 46802

FORT WAYNE'S FAMOUS CONEY ISLAND
131 W MAIN ST, FORT WAYNE, IN 46802

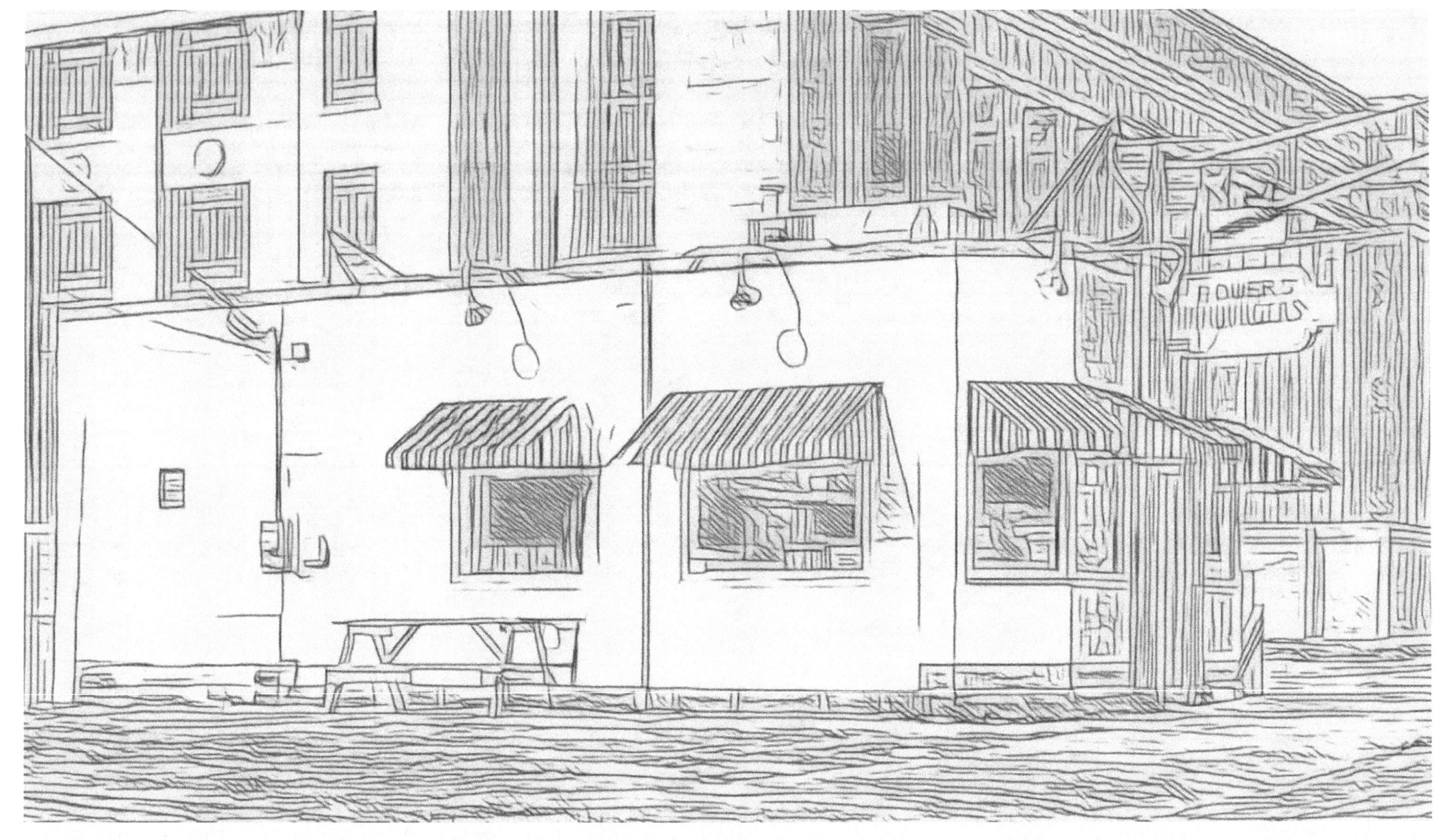

POWERS HAMBURGERS
1402 S HARRISON ST, FORT WAYNE, IN 46802

FORT WAYNE FIREFIGHTERS MUSEUM
226 W WASHINGTON BLVD, FORT WAYNE, IN 46802

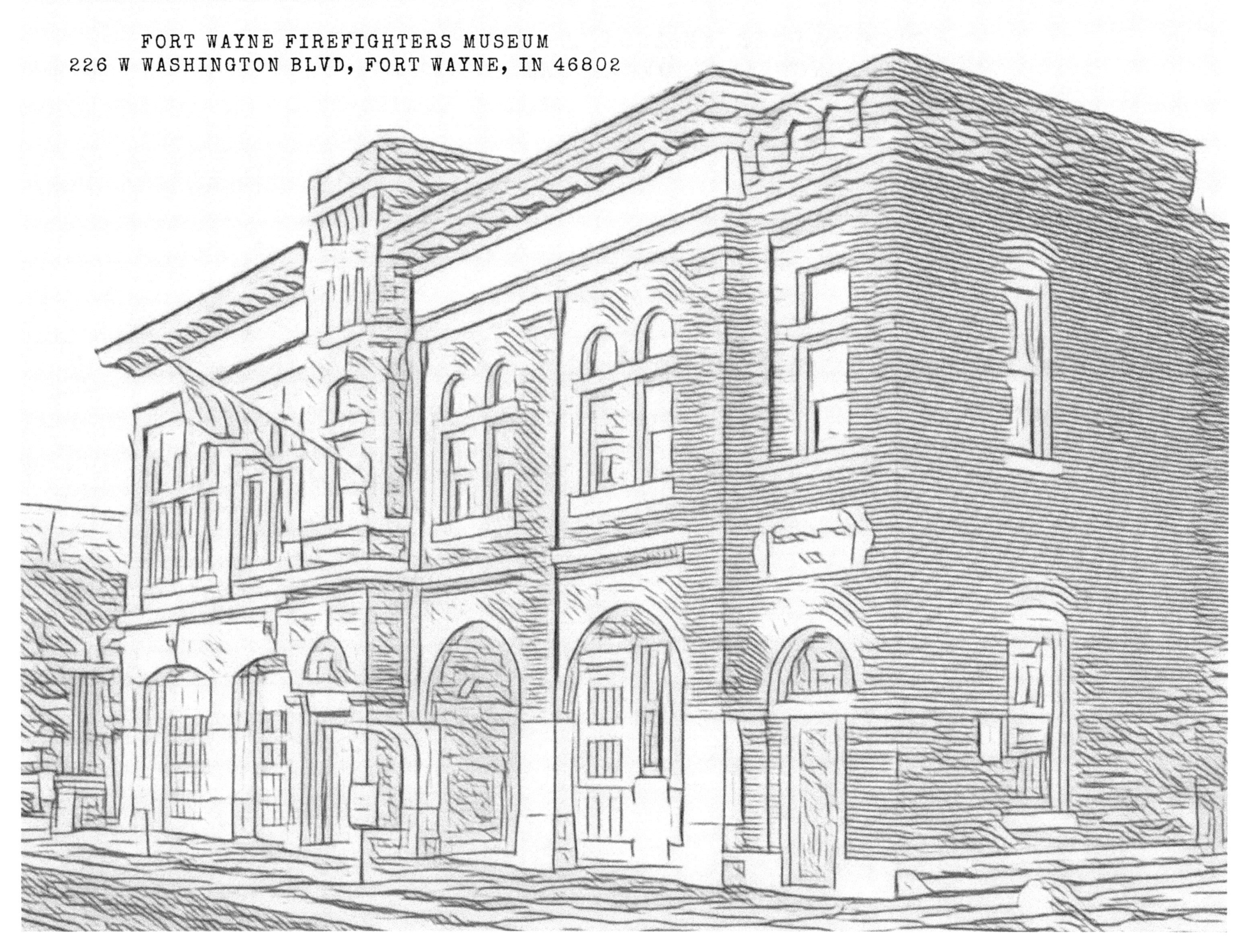

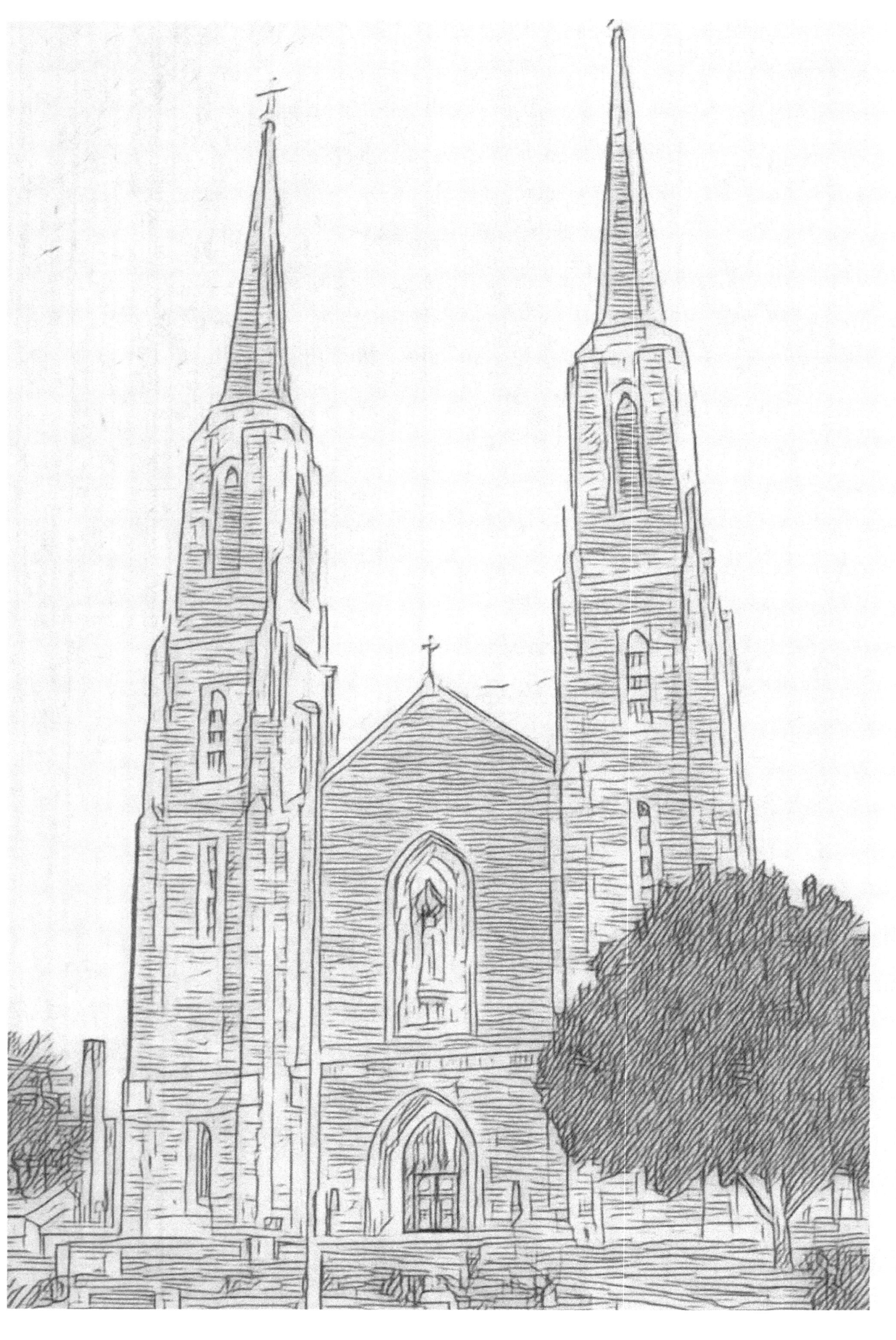

CATHEDRAL OF THE IMMACULATE CONCEPTION
1105 CALHOUN ST, FORT WAYNE, IN 46802

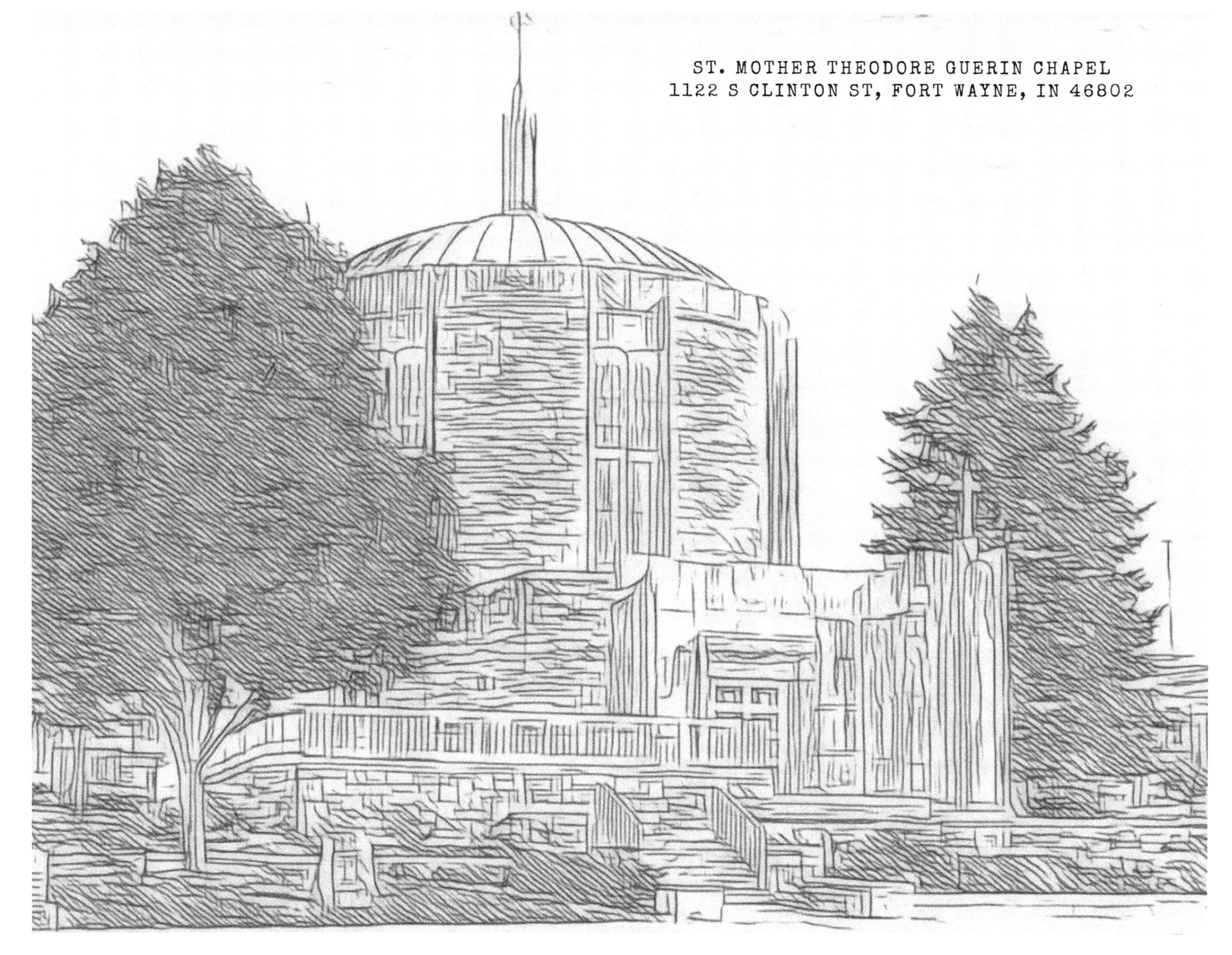

ST. MOTHER THEODORE GUERIN CHAPEL
1122 S CLINTON ST, FORT WAYNE, IN 46802

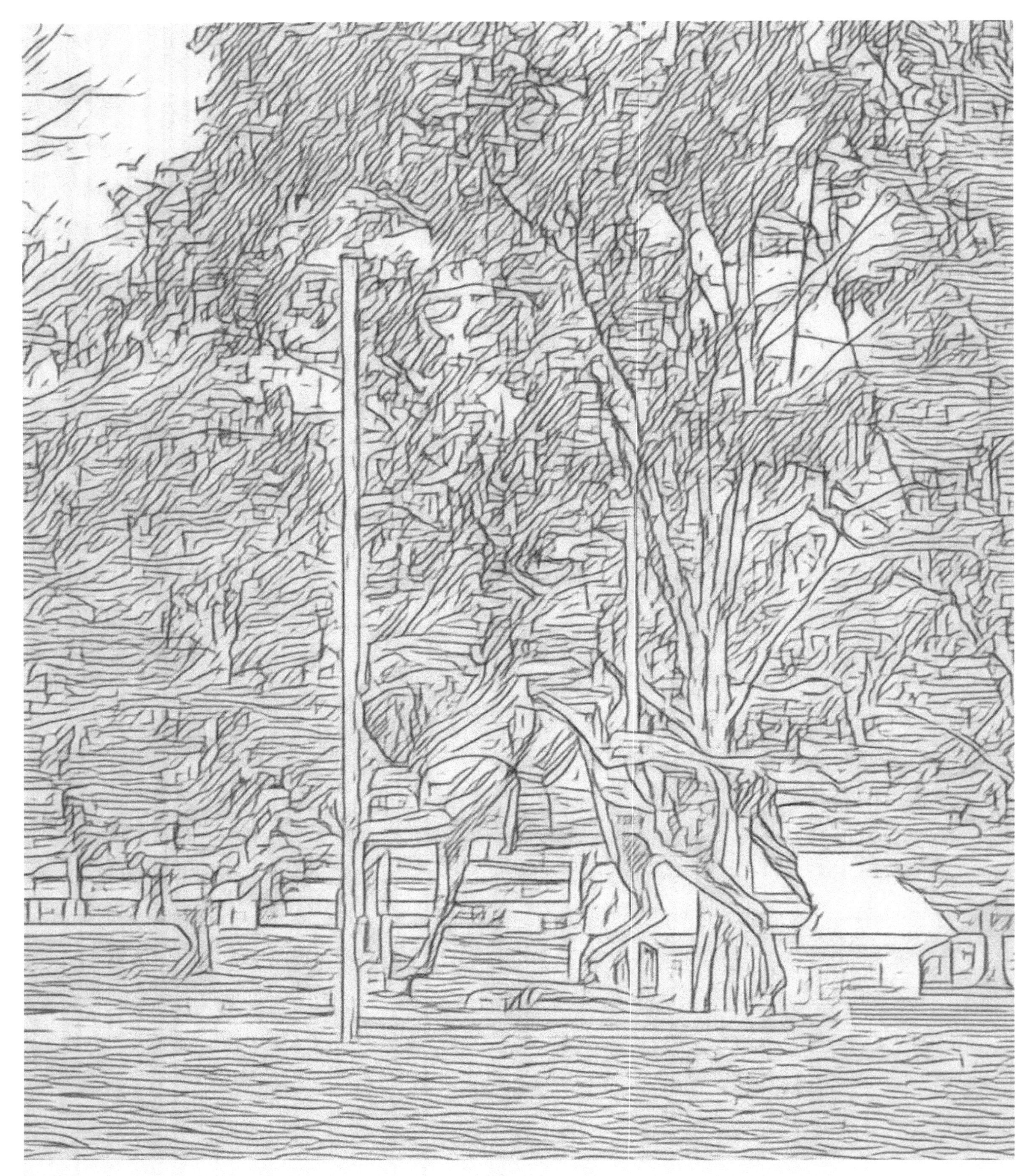

ANTHONY WAYNE STATUE AT FRIEMANN SQUARE
S CLINTON ST, FORT WAYNE, IN 46802

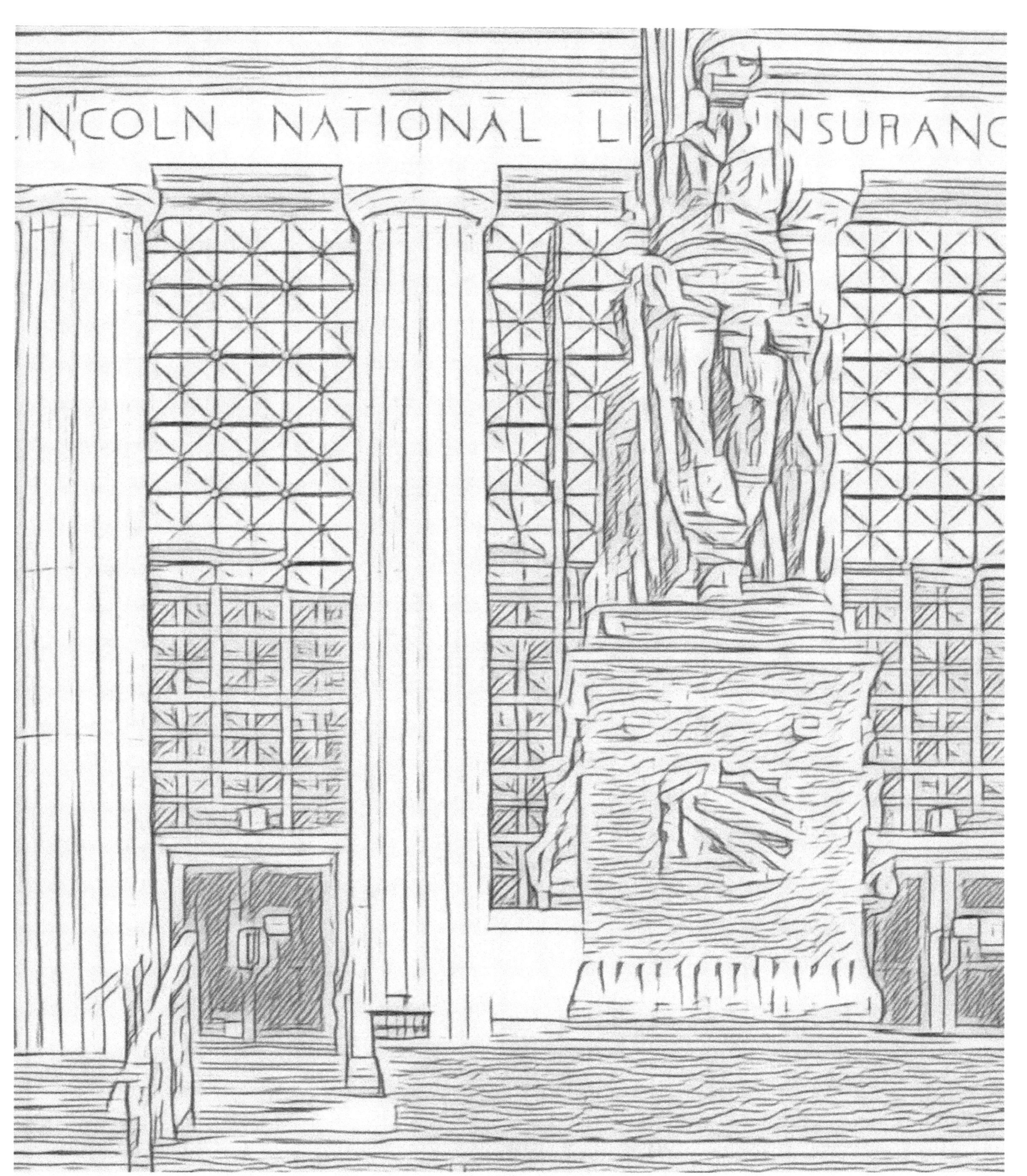

LINCOLN FINANCIAL GROUP
1301 S S HARRISON ST, FORT WAYNE, IN 46802

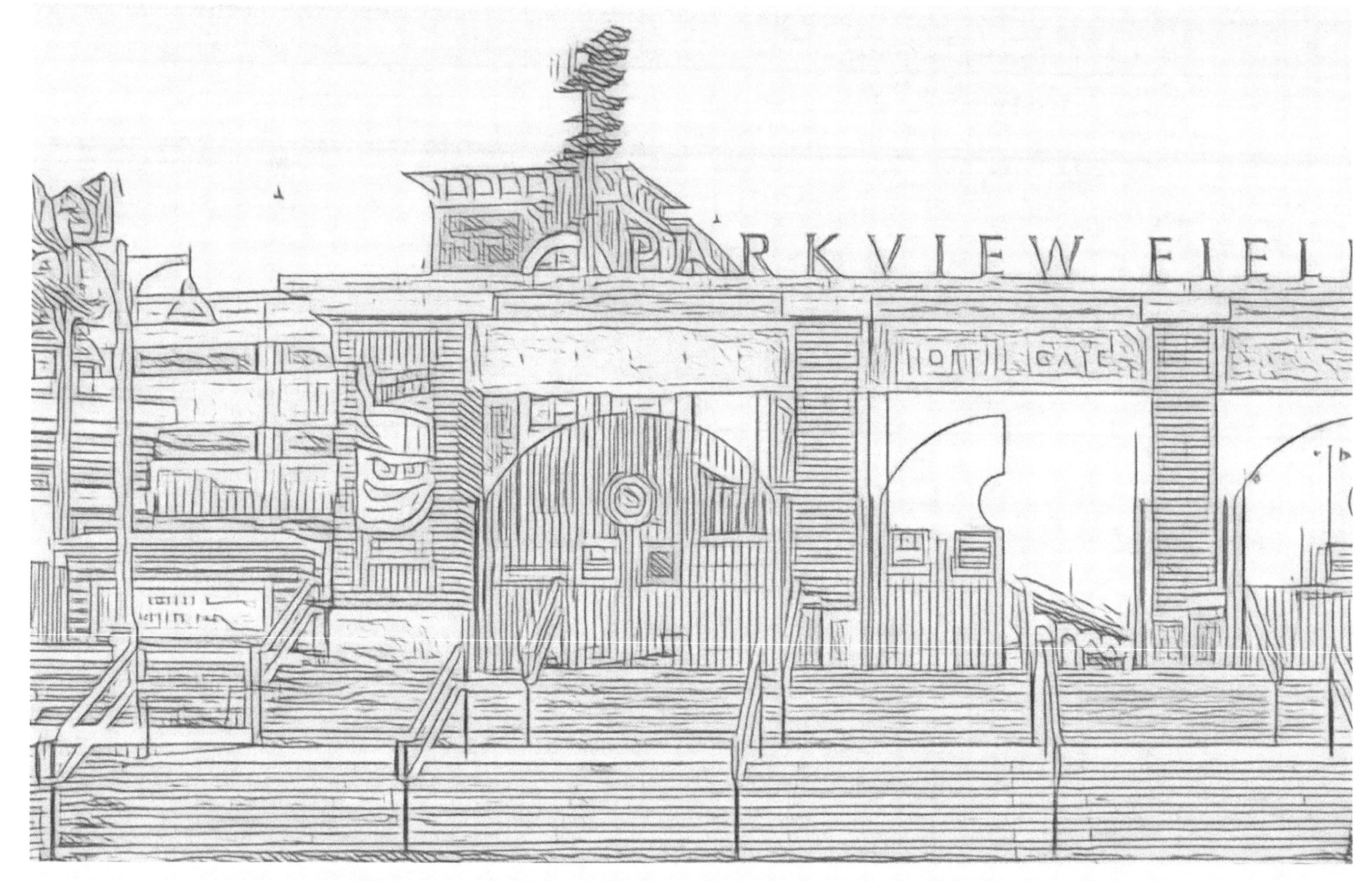

PARKVIEW FIELD, HOME OF THE FORT WAYNE TIN CAPS
1301 EWING ST, FORT WAYNE, IN 46802

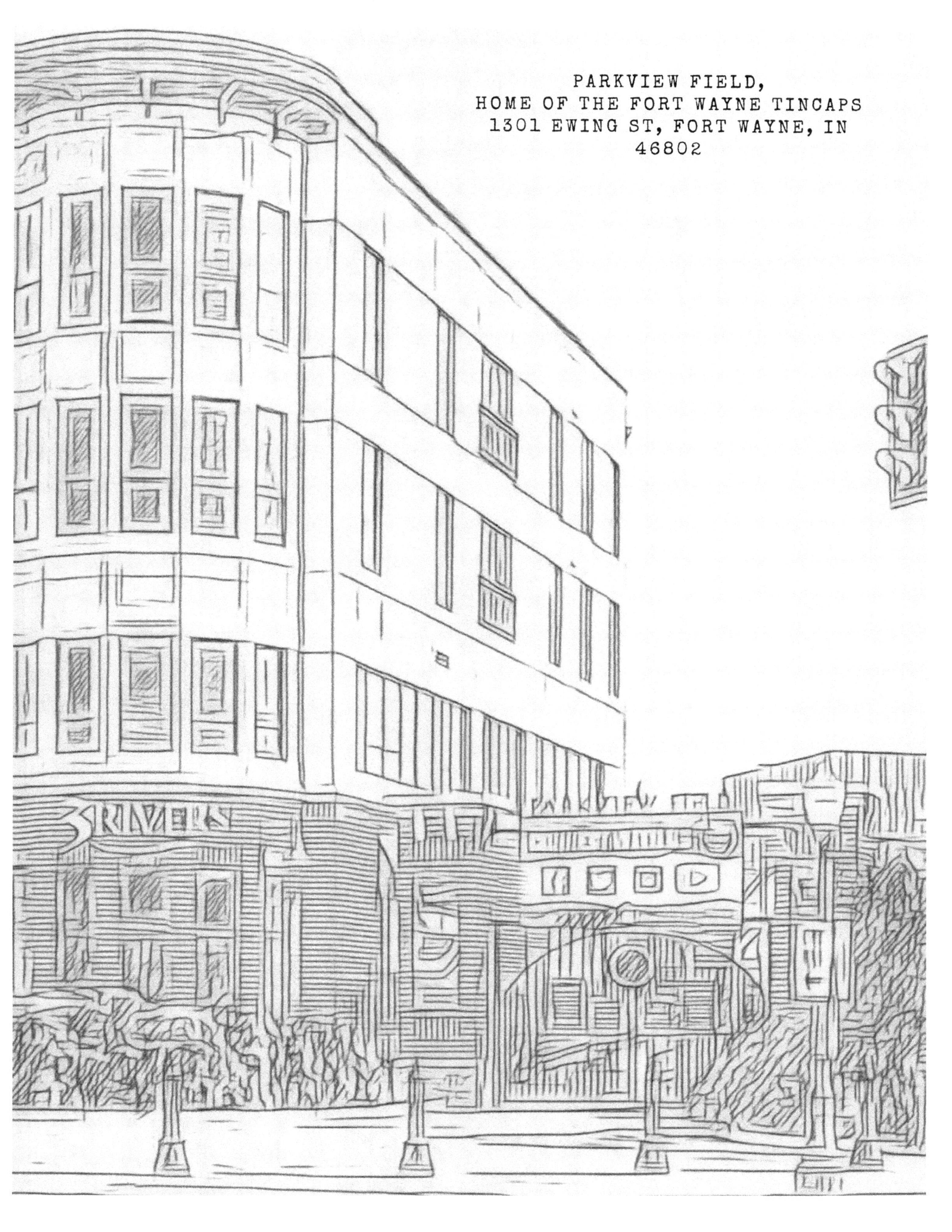

PARKVIEW FIELD,
HOME OF THE FORT WAYNE TINCAPS
1301 EWING ST, FORT WAYNE, IN
46802

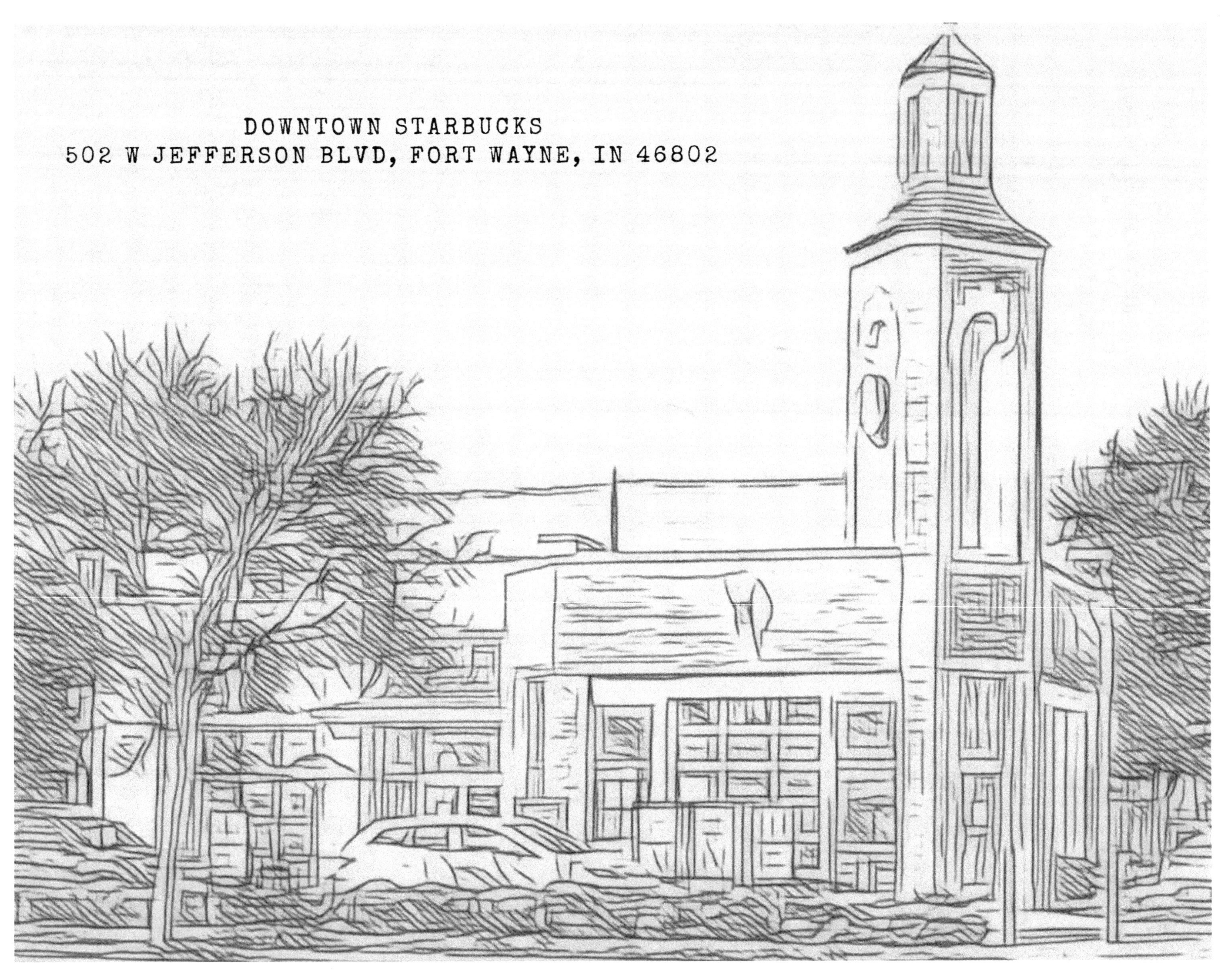

DOWNTOWN STARBUCKS
502 W JEFFERSON BLVD, FORT WAYNE, IN 46802

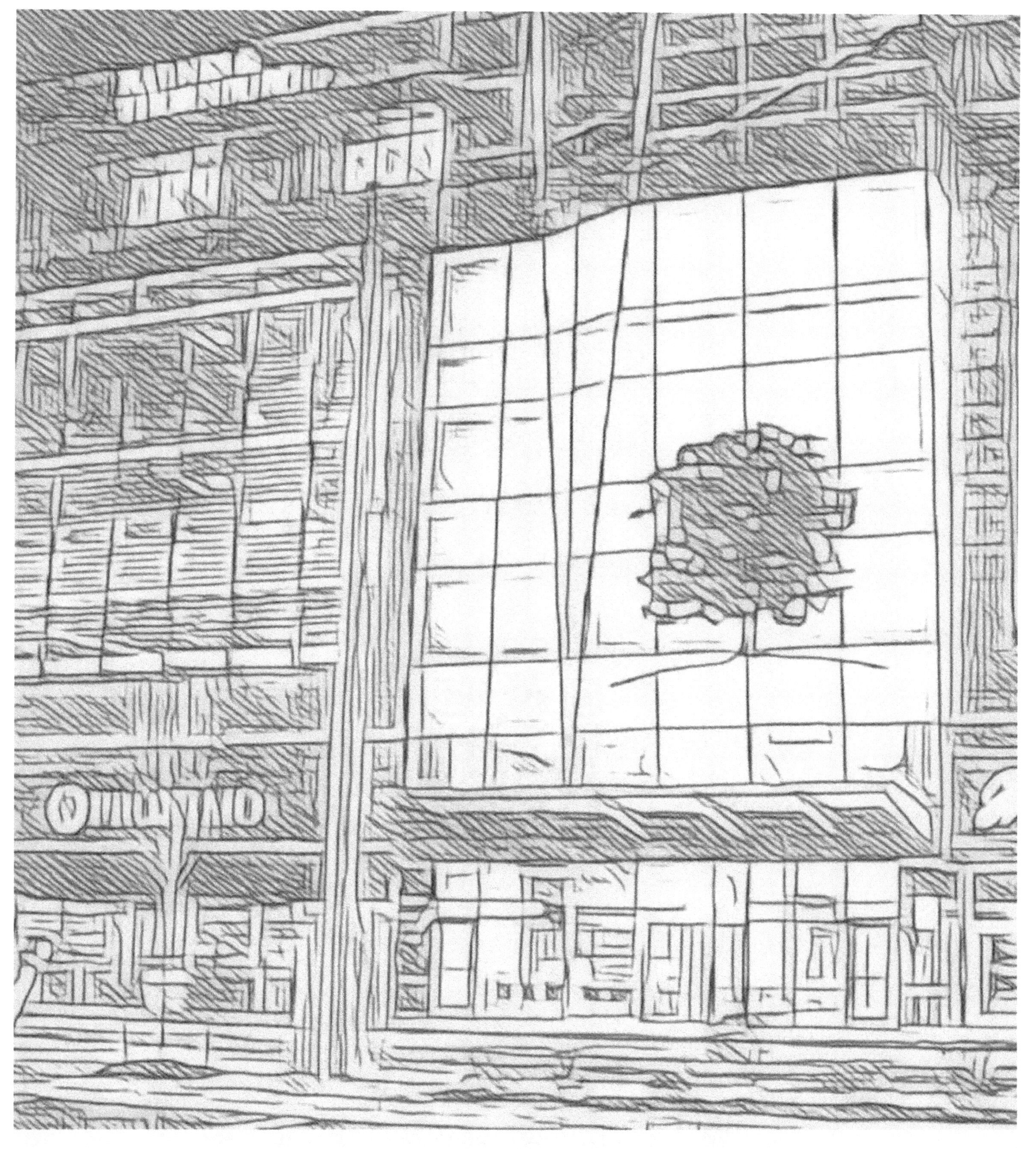

ASH BROKERAGE
888 S HARRISON ST #900, FORT WAYNE, IN 46802

SEE THE
ARTISTIC ORIGINALS

CHECK OUT THE ARTISTIC COLOR VERSIONS
OF THESE FORT WAYNE LOCATIONS IN MY
ONLINE GALLERY

LIKE THIS BOOK?

LEAVE A REVIEW AND SHARE WITH YOUR
FRIENDS!

FOLLOW MY PHOTOGRAPHY ON
SOCIAL MEDIA

INSTAGRAM @BE.PHOTOGRAPHY.INDIANA

@BE.CREATIVE.MEDIA

FACEBOOK @BE.PHOTOGRAPHY.INDIANA

@BE.CREATIVE.MEDIA

PINTEREST BEPHOTOGRAPHYINDIANA

TIK TOK @BE.PHOTOGRAPHY.INDIANA

TWITTER @BEPHOTOGRAHYIN

YOU CAN ALSO FIND MORE PHOTO ART POSTCARDS AND PRINTS IN MY ETSY SHOP

@OTISDESIGNBOUTIQUE.ETSY.COM